The Eye that Wanted to Live Alone

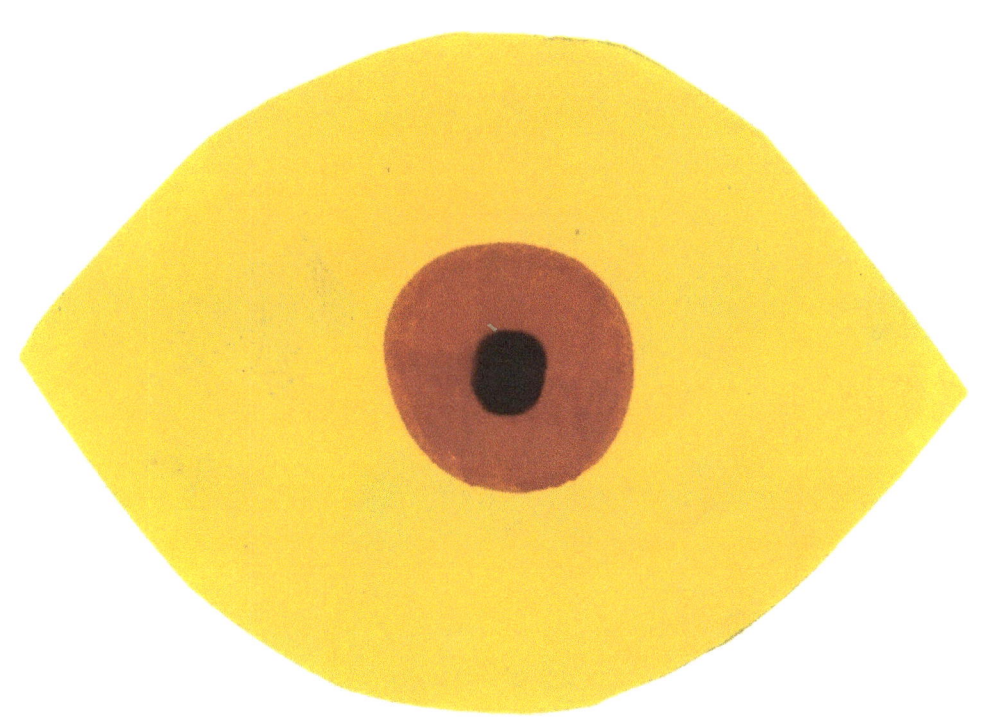

Melanie Lotfali

Once upon a time there lived
a Body. This Body had all the things
that bodies usually have,
like two eyes, two hands, tummy,
back, hair, ten fingers,
and a bottom.

The parts of the Body were different and played different roles but they all worked together successfully.

For example, when Tummy felt empty, she told Eye to look for something to eat.

Eye looked for food and then
told Hand to take it. Hand took the food,
Mouth opened and received the food.
Teeth chewed the food and Tummy received
the food. Tummy turned it into energy
which it sent to Arms and Legs
so that they could do their work.
And so, all the parts of the body worked
together in harmony.

But, one day, Eye started to think that she was more important than the other body parts.

She thought: "If I don't look for food, Hand doesn't know where to get it. Then, Mouth doesn't know to open and Tummy stays empty. I am the most important!"

Eye ordered the other body parts
to call her Queen Eye. She told them
that she was the most important
and they should honor her.
But the other body parts didn't agree.

They said to Eye: "No, we all need
each other. We all help each other
and depend on each other."

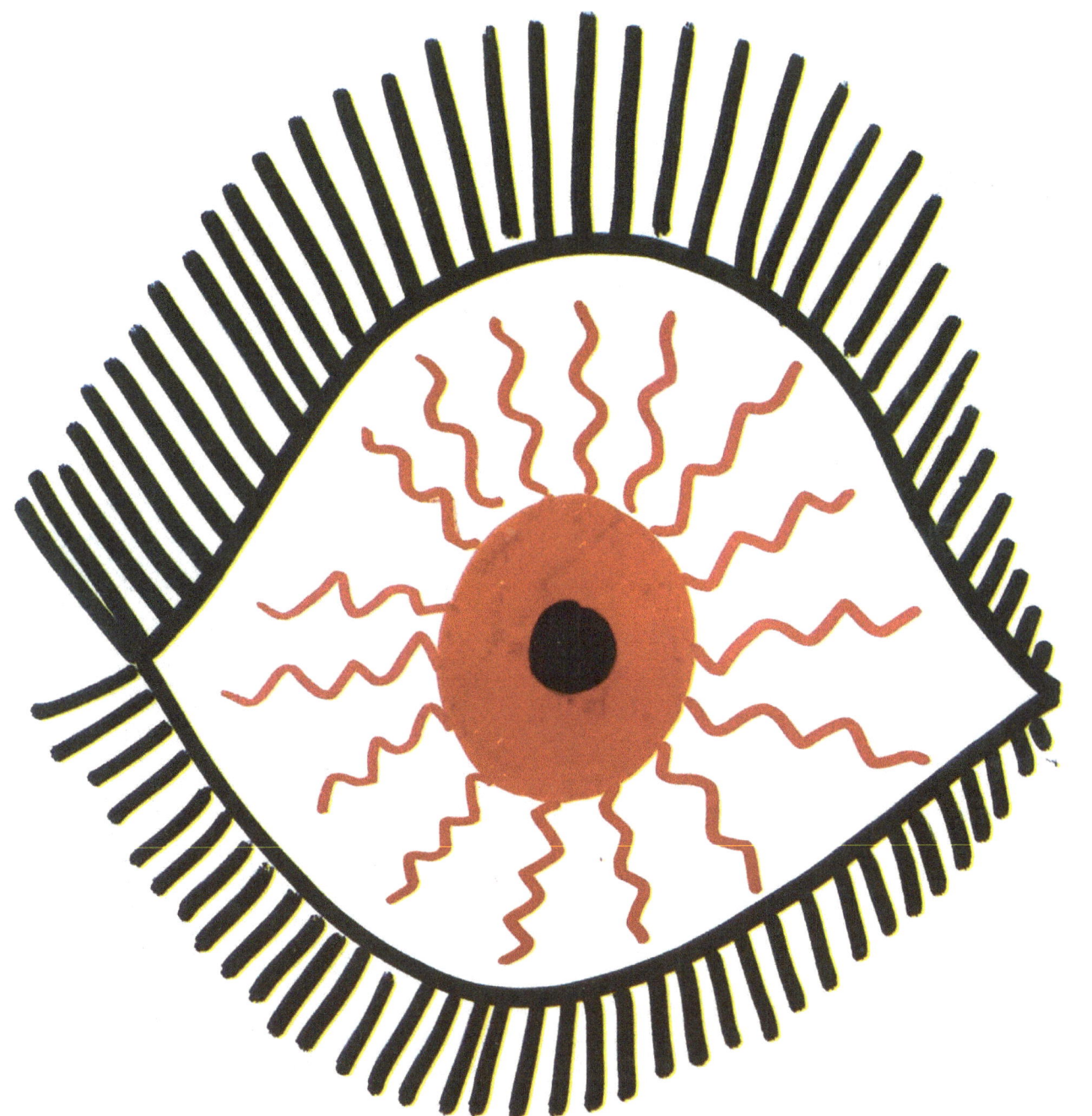

When Eye heard that they didn't accept that she was most important, she was angry!

She said: **"If you don't accept that I am queen, and if you don't honor me, I will not live with you!"**

Eye popped out of Face.
She went to live alone
on the table top.

The body parts felt very sad
that Eye didn't want to live with them.
A couple of hours later, Tummy felt empty.
She sent a message to Eye's place,
but there was no Eye. So the message
was sent directly to Hand.
Hand received the message
but didn't know what to do.
He didn't know where to find food.

Hand began to look for food by feeling.
This took a long time but in the end
he found a banana and gave it to Mouth.
Mouth received it. Teeth chewed it.
Tummy turned it into energy and
sent it to Arms and Legs.
Body suffered, but it didn't die.

Meanwhile Eye sat alone on the table top. She sat and thought about how she was more important than the other parts. But after some time she also began to lose energy. Alone she could not get food, chew it or turn it into energy.

In the end she was about to die.
She called the Body and said:
"Help me please. I am about to die."
The Body said to Eye:
"You are right. You can't live alone.
We need your help and you also need us.
Let's help each other."
Hand picked up Eye and put
her back in Face.

Eye began to receive energy
from the food that Tummy received
from Hand and Mouth. Eye didn't die.
She felt happy.

Eye said sorry to the other parts and said:
"I made a mistake. You were right.
We should all work together.
We are all important, and
we need unity to live well together."

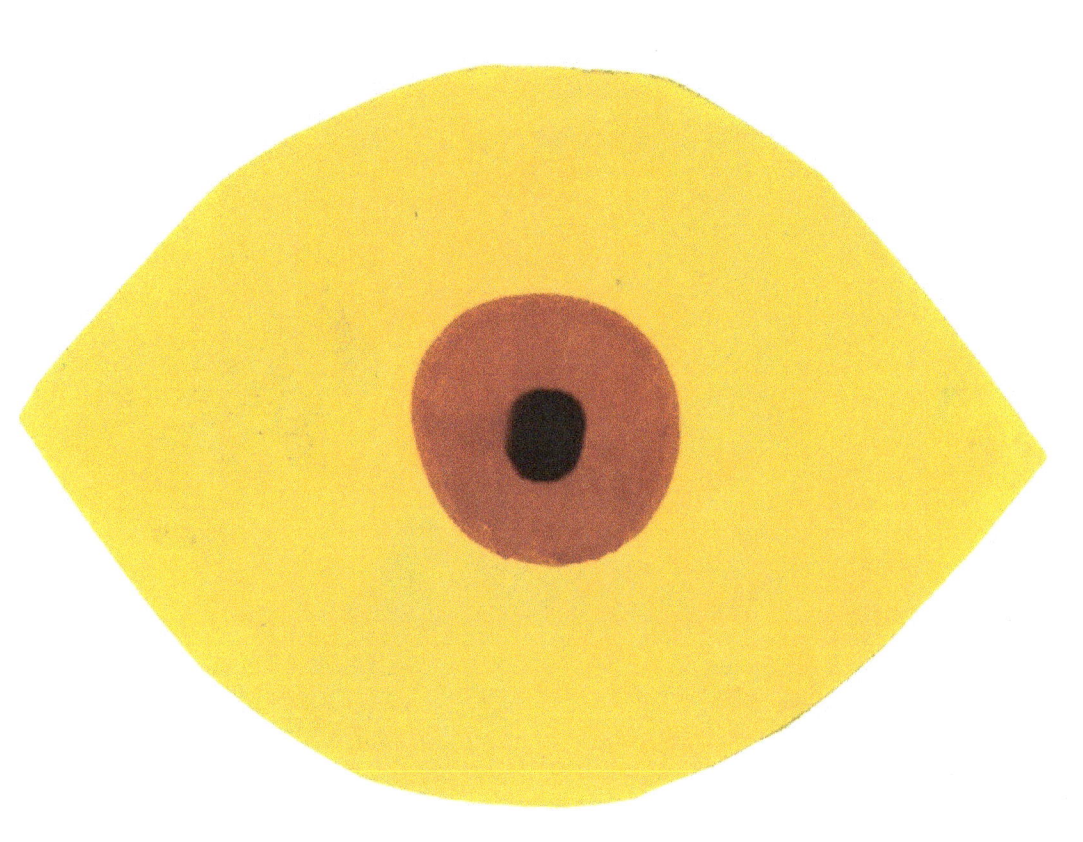

Be ye as the fingers of one hand, the members of one body.

~ Bahá'í Writings ~

Copyright © 2013 Melanie Lotfali

The Eye that Wanted to Live Alone
by Melanie Lotfali is licensed
under a Creative Commons
Attribution-NonCommercial-ShareAlike 4.0
International License.

ISBN 978-0-9945817-8-5